ROCK YOUR SKILLS

I0465436

Future skills, brought to life through music

To those who have always believed in me, to those who have learned to do so, and to those who have never done it, not even for a moment.

Too often, wisdom is nothing more than the most stagnant caution, and almost always, behind the hill, there is the sun.
Mogol

Chapter list

The Unbearable Weight of Uncertainty   5

Track #1: Give Peace a Chance - Leadership and Social Influence   8

Track #2: Wish You Were Here, Emotional Intelligence   11

Track #3: Respect, Diversity and Inclusivity Management   14

Track #4: Bohemian Rhapsody, Complex Problem-Solving   17

Track #5: Like a Rolling Stone, Change Management   20

Track #6: Good Vibrations, Creativity   22

Track #7: Dancing Queen, Storytelling   25

Track #8: Superstition, Multidisciplinarity   28

Track #9: Get Back, Stress and Conflict Management   31

Track #10: Come as You Are, Empathy   34

The Virtuous Contamination   36

The Unbearable Weight of Uncertainty

World Economic Forum, Harvard Business Review, Forbes, McKinsey—these are just a few of the organizations that have attempted to analyze the skills essential for the future workforce.

All these analyses share a fundamental premise: the skills demanded by the market are changing at an unprecedented pace. The ongoing Industry 4.0 revolution is perhaps comparable only to the first Industrial Revolution, which upended the work paradigms of its time almost overnight.

But what does Industry 4.0 mean?

We find ourselves standing at a precipice, facing a disruption driven by the rapid advancement of technology. Beyond this point, nothing will remain the same—in our daily lives and, above all, in the professional world as we know it today.

Thanks to the technological acceleration of recent years, solutions have emerged that not long ago existed only as grandiose terms in science fiction movies: Artificial Intelligence, Machine Learning, the Internet of Things, Big Data Analytics, and more.

By the time this book is published, these technologies will have already evolved, undergone profound transformations, or may even have become obsolete.

Amid this sea of uncertainty, one thing is relatively certain: within the next twenty years, numerous professions will disappear, while many others—some of which we can hardly imagine today—will emerge.

Think of influencers. If someone had told you twenty years ago that this profession would exist and that its salaries could sometimes reach six figures, you would have laughed heartily.

Today, however, at least 50% of the world envies the entrepreneurial prowess of Chiara Ferragni and her peers, while the other 50% is lying (at least to themselves).

Let's move from imagination to reality.

When we ponder which professions will certainly vanish, we immediately think of those replaceable by automation and robotics: assembly line jobs, repetitive or standardizable tasks, and the like.

This is entirely accurate—but it doesn't end there! Among the most at-risk professions, we may find some surprising candidates. Take, for instance, the taxi driver and the referee.

The Taxi Driver. A mythical figure of urban centers, the taxi driver knows their city's streets better than Google Maps, a proud guide for travelers and business people alike. Well, in the future, they may need to reinvent themselves.

In recent years, progress in the development of autonomous vehicles has been remarkable. What was mere utopia a few years ago has now entered the testing phase in various parts of the world. Soon, driverless cars will likely become a permanent part of our lives.

One of the professions most impacted by this shift will undoubtedly be that of the taxi driver, overtaken by futuristic self-driving cars equipped with virtual assistants who will ask, in dulcet tones, where we wish to go and take us there without the risk of a sleepy driver.

The Referee. The scapegoat of countless misadventures, often the undeserved target of creative insults, and the decision-maker whose calls can lead teams and entire fanbases to triumph or heartbreak. The referee, too, may need to reinvent their profession, drawing upon their years of experience on the field.

Recent advancements in soccer, for instance, have gradually diminished the referee's authority, starting with goal-line technology, which accurately detects whether the ball has crossed the line, and the introduction of the VAR (Video Assistant Referee) system.

Currently, VAR is used in specific scenarios, such as awarding goals, penalties, direct red cards, and cases of mistaken identity. VAR referees remain in constant radio communication with the on-field referee, offering suggestions for potential reviews. However, in certain objective situations, like offside calls, the technology makes the decision autonomously.

It won't happen overnight, but as artificial intelligence advances, the necessity of human judgment will diminish. Machines will increasingly make decisions devoid of the biases and emotional pressures that can influence humans.

As technology becomes increasingly unpredictable, both in its evolution and applications, we face a paradox. While we can hardly imagine what technology will be capable of, we can more easily predict what it won't do: replace humans in their deepest competencies, the so-called soft skills— qualities like creativity and empathy, which are inherently human and challenging for technology to replicate.

For future workers, developing these skills will be crucial in an unpredictable world that could transform at any moment. However, building such skills is not straightforward. Many are simply expressions of personality or natural inclinations. These aren't about learning to operate a machine but about managing emotions and cultivating distinctive traits that add value in the competitive job market.

Soft skills, when not innate, must be deliberately trained through hands-on experience and self-awareness. Unlike technical skills, which can be acquired through training or procedural learning, soft skills demand a different approach.

Developing soft skills begins with understanding them, often by translating them into observable behaviors. The key question is, "What behavior will show that I've mastered this soft skill?" Setting clear goals and indicators helps track progress.

Achieving these skills involves a cycle of testing and learning. At first, mistakes are inevitable. But over time, the melody—initially composed in our minds—gains harmonious words that guide us toward meaningful actions.

I once met Maestro Mogol, the greatest Italian lyricist of all time, who posed the question, "In a song, do the words or the melody come first?"

We amateurishly guessed it was subjective, but Mogol revealed that songs follow a logic: first comes the melody, followed by the words that bring it to life.

The same principle applies to soft skills. First, outline a clear path of concrete actions; then populate it with practical applications in daily life.

No two soft skills are alike. We can define and categorize them, but their true value lies in individual interpretation and application. Each professional should compose their personal "melody" of future competencies, drawing inspiration from proven models.

I've crafted this book as a kind of playlist—a guide to understanding the skills of the future, infused with lessons from the greatest hits of rock and beyond. Through this exploration, I hope to inspire you to write your own success story.

So sit back, relax, and start listening—oops, I mean reading!

Track #1: Give Peace a Chance - Leadership and Social Influence
"All we are saying is give peace a chance" – Plastic Ono Band.

Nine astonishingly simple words that instantly transformed into an anthem of peace, echoing in the largest squares of America and beyond, sung at the top of their lungs by young and old alike to demand peace from the Stars and Stripes government.

In May 1969, the USA was still entangled in the bloody (and at times devastating) Vietnam War, which had officially begun in late 1955 and was reaching the peak of its American intervention that year, with about 550,000 troops deployed in various military forces on the ground.
The tally of human lives lost on the battlefield was growing increasingly bitter by the day, and protests against the government, aimed at halting military operations in the Asian state, were becoming more numerous and frequently supported by prominent public figures.

Among these, leading the charge, were John Lennon and Yoko Ono, who, incidentally, had tied the knot just a few months earlier. Naturally, the two artists didn't choose a conventional form of protest but came up with their own unique approach: the so-called "bed-in," already tested a few months earlier during their honeymoon.

But what is a "bed-in"?
Etymologically, the term is nothing more than a playful twist on the term "sit-in," where, to draw attention to the object of a protest, relevant areas such as squares or points of interest are occupied. Thus, as you might imagine, in pursuit of a noble cause, the bed-in involves "occupying" a bed, staying in your room on your mattress for several days.

As mentioned, John and Yoko staged their first bed-in during their honeymoon, during the last week of March 1969, spending seven days in the presidential suite of the Hilton Hotel in Amsterdam and granting the press free access to their room.
Everyone expected the bed-in to culminate in public displays of intimacy by the couple, but instead, John and Yoko stayed in their pajamas, strictly in bed, talking incessantly about love and universal peace.

Now, let's move on to May of the same year.
The ex-Beatle and the Japanese artist had planned a second bed-in in New York City, but John was denied re-entry into the USA due to legal troubles the previous year over cannabis possession.

Plan B.
The entire initiative was relocated to the Sheraton Oceanus Hotel in the Bahamas, but after a sleepless night caused by the tropical heat, the artist couple decided to move on to Plan C: Montreal!

There, in a room at the Queen Elizabeth Hotel, they spent seven days in bed with friends and acquaintances, holding press conferences, organizing meetings, and distributing documents.

This brings us to May 31, a day that included an ordinary press conference, meetings with various peace activists, and a free hour during which John had an idea to bring a crazy thought of his to life: to record a song with improvised instruments, all with the support of a portable recorder and using his friends as a choir.

So, after handing out sheets to the group with just a few verses of a song printed on them, John picked up his guitar and began strumming the melody, singing the words to rehearse the impromptu band—the Plastic Ono Band.

Everyone was asked not only to sing along but also to keep time in any way possible, from tambourines to clapping, to tapping knuckles on tables or chairs.

With these few, improvised directions, one of the most iconic songs of all time was born: Give Peace a Chance.

This anecdote about the song's creation alone should be enough for anyone who hasn't already to listen to it, but it's only the beginning of the story.

Despite the seemingly nonsensical supporting verses, the chorus had a hypnotic quality—a blend of melody and words that embedded itself in the mind like a children's rhyme.

This beautiful simplicity, combined with the slogan-like structure, made the song a true anthem of peace just days after its release.

Crowds of pacifists poured into the streets to protest the Vietnam War, endlessly chanting the song's refrain. Those nine words encapsulate thousands of ideals and emotions, whose values are summarized in a simple concept: giving peace a chance.

Arguably, if the song hadn't been written by John Lennon and Yoko Ono and publicized through the bed-in, it likely wouldn't have become a global anthem.

And John and Yoko knew this—it's highly unlikely that it all happened by chance.

The couple leveraged their social influence, using the most effective means to reach their target audience, exercising charismatic leadership capable of mobilizing the masses, even on such challenging and delicate issues.

Leadership and social influence are thus two sides of one of the essential skills for the future of workers.

But what exactly is meant by leadership and social influence?

Being a source of inspiration and support for others, helping those around us bring out the best in themselves, will be a key factor for professional success in the future.

Today, far too often, workplace relationships are based on authority, not influence. Professional connections are closely tied to hierarchical relationships, where organizational charts are fundamental to the credibility of the names within them.

But hear this: one of the first casualties of Industry 4.0's changes will likely be organizational charts.

The organizations of the future will increasingly feature agile structures, with cross-functional, mixed teams forming and disbanding based on current projects.

As if the fall of sacred organizational charts weren't enough, tomorrow's labor market composition will include fewer permanent employees, favoring agile work relationships that will activate and deactivate based on the moment's needs. This will create a fluid market of professionals and industry experts.

In this vast organizational sea, the exercise of authority will suddenly vanish, giving way to influence and thus to those leadership and social influence skills we're discussing.

Being a credible and authentic professional, able to garner followers and sponsors, will be crucial for achieving success. Acting authoritarianly will lay the groundwork for exclusion from the competitive labor market.

Track #2: Wish You Were Here, Emotional Intelligence

"We're just two lost souls swimming in a fishbowl year after year, running over the same old ground. What have we found? The same old fears. Wish you were here." – Pink Floyd.

On July 12, 2006, in Piazza Napoleone in Lucca, one of the most significant concerts of Roger Waters' life took place. Waters, a historic former member and co-founder of Pink Floyd, performed that evening in an atmosphere described by attendees as surreal, with goosebumps a natural reaction. This was not only because of Waters' stage presence but also due to the recent passing of Syd Barrett, another founding member and historical leader of the band.

Despite the fresh loss of his former bandmate, the evening seemed to proceed under the classic "show must go on" approach. Yet, the concert was unmistakably laden with shadows. These shadows came alive shortly before performing Wish You Were Here. Roger, visibly moved in a way he had rarely been in public, dedicated the entire concert to his friend without resorting to clichés or excessive rhetoric. He simply wished Syd were there.

Syd Barrett is remembered as an eclectic artist: a singer-songwriter, guitarist, composer, and even painter. Unfortunately, he is equally well-known for his erratic behavior, which led to his departure from the group—a behavior often linked to heavy drug use and an alleged mental disorder.

The word "alleged" is key because questions about the exact nature of Syd's condition persist. Schizophrenia, bipolar disorder, and Asperger syndrome are just some of the hypotheses put forward over time. However, his diagnosis was never clarified, unlike the extensive documentation regarding his use of psychoactive drugs, perhaps the true trigger for his apparent madness.

If Syd Barrett was only active in the band for four years, how is it possible that there is such an indissoluble link between him and the success of Pink Floyd? His contribution went far beyond founding the band. His wild creativity allowed the group to take its first significant steps into the music scene through unprecedented artistic experimentation, driven by lateral thinking capable of crafting brilliant psychedelic songs.

To understand his approach, consider that Syd once claimed the band's name came to him through alien inspiration. More likely, he was inspired by the first names of his two favorite blues musicians, Pink Anderson and Floyd Council. In summary, without Syd Barrett, Pink Floyd would never have achieved success.

But why did this seemingly unbreakable bond with the band last so briefly? The answer lies in his personality and character. Syd was a one-man show. Those who watched him perform swore they saw him blend with the stage lights, becoming a natural extension of the spectacle. Perhaps he was aware of this, or maybe it was just his nature. Either way, it led him to ignore his surroundings—the music industry, concerts, record labels, and, most importantly, his relationships with the people around him, including his bandmates.

At the height of Pink Floyd's growing success, Syd began acting selfishly. The most famous anecdote recounts that once the band made it onto Britain's Top of the Pops, Syd grew intolerant of appearing on the show. After the first regular performance, he showed up in pajamas for the second and outright refused to participate by the third week, allegedly reasoning, "If John Lennon doesn't do it, why should I?"

From that point on, things spiraled downward. During concerts, he would often isolate himself by the amplifier, playing the same note repeatedly, or he would stop singing, forcing his surprised and irritated bandmates to cover his parts. Performances were canceled, more and more dates were missed, and his disruptive behavior during television appearances increased.

Roger Waters, fed up, came up with what later proved to be a brilliant solution: hiring David Gilmour, Syd's childhood friend, as a supporting guitarist. In a short time, David fully replaced Syd as lead guitarist, leaving Syd with rhythm guitar and vocals. Despite efforts to recover him, the band began gradually phasing Syd out, eventually excluding him from live performances altogether.

Before officially leaving the group in April 1968, Syd showed up unannounced at a live performance at Imperial College. Still possessing the setlist, he tried to join the stage but was refused. Sitting directly in front of Gilmour, he stared him down for the entire concert, apparently hurt by the agreement they had made months earlier that Gilmour would support him, not replace him.

After this, Syd disappeared from the orbit of Pink Floyd, who seven years later dedicated an entire album to their former bandmate—arguably their greatest work, Wish You Were Here.

What did Barrett lack to continue being the band's brilliant centerpiece—the Crazy Diamond, as his former bandmates later called him in tribute? Syd was an absolute genius, but as often happens with such minds, his selfish approach to art and relationships led to his inevitable estrangement from those who once relied on him as a golden goose.

In the future of work, those who lack what we now call emotional intelligence risk similar professional isolation. "Traditional" intelligence, measured by IQ, will remain useful but no longer sufficient.

The concept of emotional intelligence is not new. It was first introduced in 1995 by journalist and psychologist Daniel Goleman, who modernized and expanded upon earlier concepts such as social intelligence (Edward L. Thorndike, 1920) and interpersonal intelligence (Howard Gardner, 1983).

Thorndike identified social intelligence as the ability to understand and guide people, acting wisely in interpersonal relationships. Gardner emphasized the ability to recognize and distinguish others' feelings, intentions, and beliefs.

Goleman, however, owes the term to two earlier researchers, Salovey and Mayer, who had already used it in psychological studies five years prior. Nevertheless, Goleman's bestselling book gave the concept widespread recognition.

In brief, Goleman describes emotional intelligence as the ability to recognize our own feelings and those of others, to motivate ourselves, and to manage emotions positively, both internally and in relationships.

In a world where technical skills will become less relevant, emotional intelligence will serve as a critical accelerator. It will ensure perseverance in achieving goals through self-motivation, while fostering empathy, optimism, assertiveness, and hope—skills deeply human and profoundly impactful.

People will face rapid changes, technological disruptions, and constant uncertainty in the competitive economic and social landscape. Under this pressure, they will need leaders and colleagues capable of offering security to guide them toward success (and serenity).

Emotional intelligence means knowing when to push someone and when to step back. It means constantly putting yourself in others' shoes to understand the deep motivations behind their actions. It requires acting as both a professional and a psychologist, even without formal training, to read emotions, provide support, and tactfully adapt. Above all, it means being recognized as a point of reference.

Had Syd Barrett possessed strong emotional intelligence, perhaps he would have continued as the Pink Floyd frontman for years. On the other hand, his genius stemmed precisely from his unconventional personality. In the end, all we can do is appreciate the musical legacy he left behind and the heartfelt tribute paid by his former bandmates.

Track #3: Respect, Diversity and Inclusivity Management

"R-E-S-P-E-C-T, find out what it means to me" - Aretha Franklin.

What if Respect, perhaps the most important and well-known song by Aretha Franklin, wasn't written by her and her rendition was just a great cover?

In fact, the original version of the song was recorded by Otis Redding, an African-American singer who achieved only modest success during his career. Today, years after his untimely death, he is regarded as one of the main pioneers of Black music and one of the greatest singers of all time by Rolling Stone magazine.

However, his version of Respect did not achieve great success and, among other things, did not even have the same lyrics we know today.

The song was first released by Redding as a single in 1965, while Aretha Franklin, encouraged by music producer Jerry Wexler, released her personal remake two years later, in 1967.

But Redding's lyrics had a peculiarity—a distinctly male-dominant tone.
As the title suggests, the song was about respect. Yes, a big, strong man like him asking his woman for respect, literally: "But all I'm askin' is for a little respect when I come home."

Not remarkable for the time, when sexism and racism were still pervasive, but the tides were beginning to change.

By 1967, both feminist movements and protests against the discriminatory regime in the U.S. were gaining momentum.
Aretha was a proud and evident representative of both "minorities."

Looking at her personal life, we can already sense the rebellious spirit that made her the Queen of Soul.
She had two children, Clarence and Edward, in her teenage years, without ever revealing the fathers' identities.

At a time when women were expected to tend to the domestic hearth, Aretha—an ambitious, modern woman striving to become a successful singer—entrusted her grandmother to raise her boys while she pursued her dream.

In an era where a father's judgment was akin to a sentence, in 1961, Aretha married Ted White, a much older man, against her father's wishes.

Fast forward to 1967, Aretha took Redding's lyrics and turned them inside out.
For her, hearing a man ask for respect from a woman was simply unacceptable.

Black women, especially in the southern United States, were daily exploited and humiliated, often beaten.

Aretha changed the original version, adding new lines like "Take care... of TCB," where TCB stood for Take Care of Business. This phrase, commonly used in the African-American subculture of the 1960s, was not as well-known among white people.

Another crucial change was the emphatic spelling of the word Respect, as if to underline that everyone needed to understand the meaning of respect. It was a lesson for the whole world, which still had much to learn about respecting others, particularly "diverse" individuals who, in the song, were symbolized by women.

Aretha recorded the song on Valentine's Day, just two days after President Lyndon Johnson's famous speech calling for an end to racism, labeling it "man's ancient curse and modern shame." This paved the way for an executive order that expanded anti-sex discrimination legislation a few months later.

Within three months, the song skyrocketed to the top of the charts in the U.S. and other countries, giving Aretha incredible international visibility and immediately cementing her as a feminist icon.

Today, Respect ranks fifth on Rolling Stone's list of the 500 greatest songs of all time.

Through her lyrics, Aretha Franklin rode the first waves of the imminent paradigm shift regarding diversity: diversity in gender, race, religion, sexual orientation, and more.

Until the 1970s, diversity was often seen as an abomination or a flaw in the world's design. Aretha, however, understood better than anyone else the strength and beauty behind these "diversities," qualities the world had ignored until then but would come to recognize in the following decades.

Diversity and Inclusion in the Professional World
Today, inclusivity and diversity management are essential traits for successful professionals and will become even more critical in the future. In a world that is increasingly connected, where workplace boundaries will grow ever thinner, professional environments will mirror this openness, evolving in tandem.

In recent years, companies have emphasized the importance of a distinctive corporate culture, made up of unique elements and expected behaviors to which employees must align to succeed.

However, mismanaging the concept of cultural fit can be detrimental.

This term, entrenched in companies and their HR departments, often masks a desire to hire people as similar as possible to those already on board, killing the value of diversity.

Instead, companies should focus on finding individuals who add to their culture, not those forcibly aligned like bland replicas of the values on their corporate websites.

Otherwise, they risk falling into the trap of organizational monoculture, which can stifle creativity and out-of-the-box thinking—both vital for market competitiveness.

Without diversity, tomorrow's companies will struggle to survive.

Professionals of the future must develop specific skills to not only embrace diversity in all its forms but also leverage its characteristics as a distinctive value proposition.

Two of the most rapidly developing and creativity-driven areas in the world are Silicon Valley and Israel.
Both owe their unique advantages to diversity—managed virtuously.

In these cases, the coexistence of profoundly different people hasn't sparked civil wars or sustained discrimination but instead fueled innovation.

The interplay of diverse viewpoints, born of heterogeneous cultures and approaches, has created centers of technological and scientific excellence characterized by unconventional thinking and constant questioning.

Professionals must emulate this mindset, acting as miniature Silicon Valleys in their respective domains.

Inclusivity is now an accepted concept among forward thinkers, but putting it into practice is another story.

Managing diversity at an individual level means engaging effectively with everyone, empathizing with them as individuals shaped by unique experiences and socio-cultural backgrounds.

At a group level, managing diversity becomes even more crucial. Tomorrow's workplaces will revolve around collaboration among people of different ethnicities and cultures.

Through the integration of diverse perspectives, companies can unlock untapped potential, generating innovations that no individual, however brilliant, could achieve alone.

Aretha Franklin understood the power of diversity and its ability to multiply value—not just for individuals but for society as a whole.

Track #4: Bohemian Rhapsody, Complex Problem-Solving

Is this the real life, is this just fantasy? Caught in a landslide, no escape from reality. Open your eyes, look up to the skies and see" - Queen.

These lines open the six minutes of the masterpiece that is the hallmark of Queen "the greatest song of all time," as voted by millions of people across more than forty countries in a 2008 survey.

In 1975, a six-minute track was a colossal gamble. Elton John himself, when asked by John Reid (Queen's manager at the time) to hear the song, exclaimed after the first listen, "Are you crazy? Radio stations will never play it!"

But let's take a step back and start with the title: Bohemian Rhapsody.

Bohemian, referring to the French bohème subculture, symbolizing nonconformity and a free spirit. Rhapsody, a type of instrumental composition characterized by diverse musical forms and metric freedom, blending rhythms and harmonies of varying nature.
These two terms perfectly encapsulate the essence of the track—a composition that defied all conventions of the musical stage, free from constraints or clichés.

Amazingly, Freddie Mercury, the group's frontman and a creative genius, began writing the song's first verses in early 1975 on the corners of a phone book.

The method might seem odd and improvised, but Freddie already had a crystal-clear vision of the song's structure. It would consist of four distinct parts, offering listeners an unparalleled musical journey:

An a cappella intro
A ballad section
An operatic passage
A concluding hard rock segment
For the time, this concept was revolutionary: merging four songs into one while ending up with a track too long for standard radio formats.

Despite Elton John's doubts about airplay potential, Freddie Mercury was undeterred. He turned to his friend Kenny Everett, a radio DJ at England's Radio Victory, who secretly received the track. Kenny played it up to 14 times in just two days, almost continuously.

The rest is history: the song quickly gained traction, becoming a global phenomenon.

Beyond Length: Experimentation and Technical Challenges
The song's duration and genre layering were not the only groundbreaking aspects. Mercury's drive for innovation in vocal harmonization and sound experimentation were pivotal. The track captivates listeners from the first play with its magnetic vocal harmonies, a complexity never before attempted.

Take, for instance, the operatic choir midway through the song—achieved through an astonishing 180 vocal overdubs.

Yes, 180 overdubs.

This number was staggering, especially considering the time required and the methods to consolidate everything onto a single tape.

Time: Recording began in late August 1975 at Rockfield Studio 1 in Wales, following three weeks of rehearsals. Sessions lasted six weeks, making A Night at the Opera (the album featuring the song) one of the most expensive albums in music history.

Method: Given the 180 layered vocal parts, existing tape technology couldn't support the ambition of such a project.

But Freddie saw the track as the culmination of his talent—a six-minute opus encapsulating his artistic vision, one he might have known would later be crowned "song of the century."

The technical recording limitations weren't going to stand in his way. Freddie, his bandmates, and the studio experimented tirelessly. They found a solution by manually cutting and splicing sections of tape with adhesive, ensuring every track fit onto the reel and delivered the masterpiece we know today.

The challenges didn't stop after the track's release, which quickly topped the charts. Queen was invited to perform on Top of the Pops, a weekly show presenting the best-selling records.

Artists typically performed live or in playback, but the layered vocals made live performance impossible, while playback would result in an awkward show with mismatched audio and lip movements.

This presented yet another complex problem. But where challenges arise, so do opportunities and groundbreaking solutions.

Queen invented the music video. They commissioned Bruce Gowers, a TV director, to create a video for the single to broadcast on Top of the Pops. It was an instant hit. From that point on, music videos became a staple for every major release.

This song embodies thinking outside the box. It's a triumph of creativity and innovation, overcoming seemingly insurmountable challenges to achieve its goal.

In the near future, the ability to solve complex problems will be one of the most sought-after skills. While technology and automation can handle routines and simple, structured problems, they cannot yet replicate human creativity.

What does complex problem-solving really mean? Imagine a 17th-century chest of drawers with countless compartments of various sizes, each holding tools for solving simple, linear problems.

Have a problem? Open one drawer to find what you need.
Have a multi-faceted problem? Open several drawers and combine their contents.
But what happens when you face a problem that none of the drawers can solve?

An algorithm might return an error or suggest a near-optimal but ultimately useless solution. Here is where human creativity shines: the ability to cross-reference information, utilize available tools (or invent new ones), and test unprecedented solutions.

Our brains are enormous toolboxes filled with knowledge, experiences, and intuition. Future professionals will tackle highly complex problems requiring the integration of direct and indirect information, lived experiences, and innovative thinking.

The approach shifts from "puzzle logic"—finding the pieces needed to complete a picture—to "patchwork logic," piecing together seemingly unrelated parts into a cohesive solution.

Confronting such problems can feel daunting, like sinking in quicksand with no apparent escape. Overcoming this initial frustration is key, using rationality to pursue a viable solution through a test and learn approach:

Test an idea
Learn from the outcome
Adjust until the right solution emerges
The second attempt will always feel easier—and perhaps even enjoyable.

Had Freddie Mercury given up at the first hurdle, without leveraging his complex problem-solving abilities, we wouldn't have Bohemian Rhapsody—nor perhaps the concept of the music video itself.

Track #5: Like a Rolling Stone, Change Management

"How does it feel, how does it feel? To be without a home, like a complete unknown, like a rolling stone"

Like a Rolling Stone is perhaps Bob Dylan's most famous track, an immediate hit that climbed the global charts less than a month after its release in June 1965.

Many recognize its melody and lyrics, but not everyone knows this song was a pivotal moment for Dylan—a turning point where he transitioned from being the king of folk music to becoming a rock icon.

At just 18, Bob Dylan began exploring the world of folk music after reading the autobiography of Woody Guthrie, considered a symbol of American protest translated into song.
At 19, in 1960, he moved to New York, where he met Joan Baez, already a star at the time. He started performing for audiences, initially living in the shadow of Baez, who soon became his partner.

Between 1962 and 1963, Dylan rose to fame, writing ballads inspired by Woody Guthrie. These songs captured the growing anger of the era, especially among youth-led protest movements.

Blowin' in the Wind and Masters of War are just two of the countless hits Dylan released in a short time. Without realizing it, he became the emblem of these movements and the voice of a generation's thoughts through his music.

In the summer of 1963, Dylan joined the great March on Washington with Joan Baez. Together, they performed on the same stage where Martin Luther King Jr. delivered his iconic "I Have a Dream" speech. Dylan had become the symbol of protest—a prophet the youth looked to for guidance in their historic struggle, channeling their aspirations through his songs.

Yet, he didn't feel the cause was his own. Even more so, he didn't want it to be. Years later, Joan Baez succinctly summarized the situation: "He didn't want to be someone people turned to." Dylan had become part of something he didn't fully represent. Breaking free from this role was challenging but not impossible, especially for him.

Dylan decided to leave behind this distorted image of a politically engaged singer-songwriter. To do so, he radically changed his music and lyrics, revealing the spontaneous and emotional musician and poet within. Out went the acoustic guitar—his trademark—for the electric guitar.

The inspiration for this shift came in 1965 during a tour in England, ironically while rehearsing songs with Joan Baez. One of these songs was an old country ballad made famous by Hank Williams, whose prophetic lyrics said, "I'm a rolling stone all alone and lost. For a life of sin, I've paid the cost…"

This experience spurred Dylan to write Like a Rolling Stone, channeling his feelings into every verse through metaphors and imaginary characters. Together, they painted a poignant picture of his state of mind.

Dylan later admitted that writing the song was like a long vomiting session. His persistent bitterness was so raw that it felt honest, even though, in the end, it wasn't hatred but a form of vengeance against a world in which he had felt trapped.

The song's protagonist, Miss Lonely, is a young woman from a privileged background. After falling from grace, she faces life's bitterness marked by loneliness and disillusionment. Having spent years mercilessly looking down on everything from her pedestal, she now begs for survival. The "rolling stone" becomes a metaphor for abandonment and inertia in the downward spiral of life.

The song emphasizes the importance of seeking freedom—a freedom that lies outside the conventional, predictable paths of American life at the time. Yet, to find or rediscover one's way, one must get lost, face failures, and find redemption, living through moments of profound despair, just like Miss Lonely.

With Like a Rolling Stone, Dylan broke free artistically, dismantling the traditional structures of pop music and reshaping them into an independent form of rock balladry. His music became a vehicle for an adult, intellectual audience—the exact opposite of what record labels sought at the time.

This courage to embrace change solidified Dylan's legacy. His melodies became timeless, and while hindsight may make it seem easy, it certainly wasn't for him in those moments.

Many tout the importance of embracing change in life and work, or even proactively seeking it. Yet, between saying and doing lies an ocean of fear, doubt, and laziness.

Let's be honest: nothing is harder than change. Yet, managing it—Change Management—will be one of the most critical skills for the future workplace.

The stability paradigms of the last century—steady jobs, lifelong careers at a single company, or even sticking to one profession—have collapsed. Today, these ideas are prehistoric, and those who fail to adapt are left behind.

This new reality demands that workers not only embrace change but proactively seek it as a constant process of self-improvement.

Professionals must keep themselves updated through self-directed learning. Modern and future technologies provide abundant resources to learn and grow, often for free. Networking and staying engaged with the outside world are vital for preparing for change.

Beyond personal adaptation, managing change within organizations will also be crucial. Technological disruptions will force companies to continuously rethink their processes. Professionals will need to actively propose and lead these transformations, rather than passively waiting for directives from above.

Had Bob Dylan rested on the laurels of his early success and conformed to the expectations placed upon him, his career might not have been as illustrious and enduring. His journey reminds us that success lies in the courage to change, even when it seems daunting.

Track #6: Good Vibrations, Creativity

"Close my eyes, she's somehow closer now, softly smile, I know she must be kind, when I look in her eyes she goes with me to a blossom world" - Beach Boys.

Good Vibrations is a masterpiece.
This is not a subjective opinion but an objective fact, confirmed by its position at number six on Rolling Stone's list of the 500 greatest songs of all time.

Let's start with the title.
Brian Wilson, founder and principal songwriter of the Beach Boys, attributed the inspiration for the evocative title to his mother in his autobiography. She frequently reminded him during his childhood that all living beings—whether animals or plants—can perceive vibrations.
Wilson's creative mind and sensitive soul took this idea further, translating it into the almost utopian concept of generating positive vibrations through music to uplift listeners.

Achieving this goal required more than an ordinary song. Wilson and his bandmates needed creativity to transform the way records were made, how they could sound, and the words they could contain.
To achieve this, they used four different recording studios, each enhancing various musical elements. Seventeen sessions were spread over several months, resulting in 90 hours of recorded tape.
Ninety hours for a song lasting less than four minutes.

Each session lasted at least three hours—a near-crazy investment for a single song—risking the possibility that its various parts might not eventually converge into a coherent track. Recording costs ranged between $50,000 and $75,000, a record-breaking amount at the time.

This enormous investment in time and money was driven by the desire to experiment with a groundbreaking recording technique: the so-called "modular music" method.
This technique involved assembling different sections of a song into a sort of sound collage. This pioneering approach would later inspire the Beatles, notably in Strawberry Fields Forever and A Day in the Life. Paul McCartney himself admitted to being influenced by Brian Wilson's production style.

The crowning achievement of the band's experimentation was their use of alternative or obsolete instruments, such as the Electro-Theremin.
The Electro-Theremin is a modernized, simplified version of the older Theremin, an instrument invented in 1919 by Soviet physicist Léon Theremin. The original instrument relied on oscillators and the physical principle of beat frequency, producing sound by positioning hands in its wave field.

The Electro-Theremin, by contrast, is a small electric keyboard that mimics the sound of its predecessor through two metal antennas about a meter apart. These antennas generate sound as the player moves their hands between them, adjusting pitch and volume.
This musical indulgence was costly: recording with the Electro-Theremin alone cost $15,000.

While the music demanded such effort and resources, the lyrics were written in just five minutes by Mike Love, Brian Wilson's cousin. Inspiration struck while he was driving with his pregnant wife, Suzanne, who dutifully transcribed the words as he dictated.

Through their extreme creativity, Brian and his bandmates produced their most innovative single—Good Vibrations—the Beach Boys' best-selling track. Over a million copies were sold in the United States alone, with more than 200,000 flying off shelves within four days of release.

Often, successful songs result from a composer's brilliant intuition, vision, or introspection. But Good Vibrations is different.
It is a product of deliberate artistic awareness, driven by curiosity and aimed at creating something the world had never seen.

Creativity is the cornerstone of this song—and the future of work.

More than a skill, creativity is a critical asset for organizations, the added value that ensures survival and success. Thankfully, technologies and artificial intelligence cannot yet compete with humans in terms of creativity—at least not for now.

The future job market will demand new ways of thinking, with human creativity as the key. But what exactly is creativity?

First, let's clarify what it is not: creativity is not art. Art is merely one of the many ways creativity can be expressed.

Creativity is a skill closely linked to problem-solving but distinguished by its innovative, original nature. This originality will be vital not only for solving problems but also for innovating products and processes.
Creativity, therefore, is the engine of innovation.

In an era of technological disruption, the markets for products and services are becoming increasingly competitive. Innovation is—and will remain—the only recipe for survival. Those unable to innovate will inevitably fail and be excluded from the competition.

Organizations will increasingly seek people capable of driving and activating creative processes. Creativity involves having the courage to abandon outdated approaches and take calculated risks.

Creativity is not a genetic trait; it is a matter of stimuli—stimuli that we can nurture and train in various ways.

In recent years, many new approaches to creativity have emerged, facilitating the mental processes behind creative thinking. Two of the most well-known and effective methods are lateral thinking and design thinking.

Lateral thinking, developed by Maltese psychologist Edward de Bono, involves solving problems by approaching them from different angles rather than the direct, vertical thinking typically used to find solutions.
Lateral thinking challenges logical conventions, seeking alternative perspectives to generate out-of-the-box solutions and achieve innovation through unconventional paths.

Design thinking, on the other hand, is an iterative process where assumptions are repeatedly challenged and problems are redefined to identify alternative solutions that are not immediately evident. This approach—typically carried out in small groups—reveals unexpected ideas full of innovation or previously hidden solutions.

The good news is that creativity can be trained and is not synonymous with genius. Anyone can tap into their creative potential if properly stimulated, especially through collaboration with people who have diverse perspectives and personalities.

Creativity will be crucial for anyone aspiring to be a sought-after professional in tomorrow's job market. The time to cultivate its foundations is now.

Many attribute Good Vibrations to Brian Wilson's genius, but the song is more likely the result of his determined creativity. Without his persistence in testing new solutions, combined with the study and reinvention of older techniques like the Theremin, the Beach Boys might have produced successful songs—but never a masterpiece like Good Vibrations, a symbol of creativity and originality.

Track #7: Dancing Queen, Storytelling

"Ooh, you can dance, you can jive, having the time of your life. Ooh, see that girl, watch that scene, digging the dancing queen" – ABBA.

Dancing Queen is one of the biggest hits released by ABBA, the Swedish band that revolutionized the pop and disco-dance music scene in the 1970s, a time when it was rare for non-English-speaking groups to achieve such widespread success in English-speaking countries.

Dancing Queen was neither ABBA's debut track nor perhaps their most groundbreaking, but it is undoubtedly remembered as their most iconic, thanks to the magical story surrounding it—or rather, the magical story the band was able to build around it.

After their major victory at the 1974 Eurovision Song Contest with the song Waterloo, the band needed to quickly record a new album. The group's two composers, Björn Ulvaeus and Benny Andersson, locked themselves in a house in the suburbs of Stockholm for two days, writing melody after melody.

An interesting tidbit: the name ABBA derives from the initials of the band members' first names—the two "B's" belong to Björn and Benny, while the "A's" represent the two women in the group, Agnetha Fältskog and Anni-Frid Lyngstad, though the latter is better known simply as Frida.

After two intense days, Björn and Benny emerged with three melodies that would form the basis for two new songs, Fernando and, of course, Dancing Queen. The third melody, however, remained unreleased.

Another fun fact: for a time, the band members were also two real-life couples—Benny was dating Frida, while Björn was with Agnetha.

It was Benny who first privately played the melody of Dancing Queen for Frida, and she was so moved that she burst into tears.

However, the melody needed lyrics, and it took months to craft a version everyone was satisfied with. Björn and the band's manager, Stig Anderson, collaborated on this, with Anderson also coming up with the song's title.

By early 1976, ABBA had two fresh songs ready to release: Fernando and Dancing Queen. Both had enormous commercial potential, though they were quite different in style—Fernando was a ballad, while Dancing Queen was an upbeat disco-dance track.

From a marketing perspective, it was crucial to release one at a time. The group's manager decided on Fernando first, aiming to alternate the style of their singles; their last hit, Mamma Mia, had been a very rhythmic track.

So, despite having been previewed on some TV shows, Dancing Queen had to wait until June 18, 1976, for its official release—a very special occasion.

Back in 1972, a then-unknown Silvia Sommerlath took a job as a hostess at the Munich Olympics, a gig to supplement her finances.

Silvia, born in Germany during World War II to a German father and Brazilian mother, spent her childhood in Brazil, where her father had moved for work. The family returned to Germany in 1957, and Silvia, leveraging her bilingual upbringing, aspired to become an interpreter.

Over time, she mastered not only German and Portuguese but also French and English, which helped her secure jobs in international settings, aided by her unmistakable elegance and undeniable beauty.

At the 1972 Olympics, Silvia caught the eye of an elite guest who couldn't stop staring at her: Carl Gustaf, the Crown Prince of Sweden. He began courting her immediately, and within days, he managed to secure a first date.

The two started dating, and a year later, Carl became Sweden's new king following the death of his grandfather.

Over the next few years, their relationship blossomed. Silvia eventually moved to Stockholm and, in March 1976, accepted Carl's proposal. The couple announced their wedding, set for three months later in June 1976 at Stockholm Cathedral.

At the same time, the group was recording Dancing Queen. As mentioned earlier, the song had massive potential, but it needed a grand launch to secure its success.

What better occasion than the royal gala the night before the King and Sweden's future Queen's wedding?

So, the track debuted on live TV and was dedicated to the future queen, becoming the Swedish royal couple's song.

One might think the song was inspired by the queen herself, but that wasn't the case. The lyrics tell the story of a seventeen-year-old girl enjoying a fleeting moment of happiness on the dance floor, blissfully unaware of the future ahead—a far cry from Silvia's situation at the time, as she hardly considered her future to be "unknown"!

But ABBA's genius lay in crafting a story around the song, one that had no actual connection to its lyrics. The launch was monumental, and to this day, Dancing Queen is inextricably linked to Sweden's queen, all thanks to the storytelling prowess of the Nordic quartet.

Yes, ABBA needed a story to best communicate what was already a likely hit, and the tale of a common girl meeting her prince and living happily ever after was perfect.

Telling a story doesn't mean inflating trivial matters with words. It means finding the most effective way to communicate an idea.

Storytelling captivates attention and conveys key concepts more effectively by engaging the audience on both psychological and emotional levels.

In simpler terms, it's the ability to present ideas in a way that resonates with your audience, whether it's a speech audience, colleagues in a meeting, or a recruiter during a job interview.

Many companies have already embraced "corporate storytelling," using effective communication strategies to convey their brand messages through distinctive, relatable narratives.

This trend will only grow, becoming increasingly important in the workforce for professionals at all levels.

Storytelling will be a valuable skill throughout one's career, from entering the job market to advancing professionally. It will become essential for presenting resumes, delivering engaging communications, showcasing business results, or negotiating sales deals.

But let's be clear: storytelling doesn't mean lying. It means "dressing" an idea in the most effective way, structuring it so that it's easily understood, especially when paired with anecdotes or memorable stories.

Whether we realize it or not, everyone in the business world now tells stories in countless ways. Developing this skill can be the difference between thriving in your career or stalling, even if you possess strong technical skills.

Technical professions like ICT specialists, financial analysts, and engineers often struggle to explain their work to those outside their fields. Without storytelling, their contributions may never gain the recognition they deserve.

Being skilled in your field is no longer enough; you must also know how to articulate it.

Storytelling involves stripping away jargon and technical terms, imagining you're presenting to a child or elderly person. This "conceptual cleanup" is followed by creating a narrative that serves as a Trojan horse, embedding your message in your audience's mind.

While quirky business stories, unusual anecdotes, and personal tales are popular tools, they come with risks. They can either oversimplify the message or confuse the audience if the story isn't clearly tied to the concept.

In this book, I've tried to use storytelling to explain the future skills needed in the workforce—a potentially dry and complex topic—by relating it to the greatest successes in music.

ABBA's phenomenal impact was undeniable, with or without storytelling. However, Dancing Queen wouldn't have become a global evergreen if the Swedish band hadn't seized the opportunity to connect it with one of the most captivating narratives ever: the story of a common girl meeting her prince and living happily ever after.

Track #8: Superstition, Multidisciplinarity

"When you believe in things that you don't understand, then you suffer, Superstition ain't the way" – Stevie Wonder.

For many reasons, Superstition is perhaps the most important song ever written by Stevie Wonder.

The track was the first single released from the phenomenal Talking Book album, published in 1972, which won two Grammy Awards in 1973 for Best R&B Song and Best R&B Vocal Performance.

This song marked a turning point for Stevie Wonder, introducing a new style that would accompany him for the rest of his career.

He abruptly moved away from the pop style of the Motown Sound—soul music characterized by the use of bass, distinct melodic structures and arrangements, and a unique vocal style—to embrace melodies and musical rhythms leaning more toward funk, using simpler and repetitive structures and frequently incorporating synthesizers.

Behind Superstition lies a curious anecdote: initially, the song was meant to be recorded by Jeff Beck, as Stevie Wonder had directly promised him. However, as often happens in such cases, the record label intervened. The CEO of Wonder's label, taking advantage of Beck's delay in releasing the track, insisted that Stevie record it himself.

The collaboration between Beck and Wonder originated from Beck's public admiration for Wonder, which, when Stevie learned about it, led him to invite Beck to participate in the recording sessions for Talking Book.

In return for Beck's guitar accompaniment on some tracks, Wonder promised to gift him one of his songs—Superstition.

The song was actually born almost by chance. Beck was improvising a drum rhythm when Stevie suddenly entered the recording studio and was struck by the melody. He asked Beck to keep playing, and thus, the iconic opening lick of the song came to life.

As you might imagine, Beck wasn't thrilled with how things turned out. However, in an attempt to make amends, Stevie gifted him another song, Cause We've Ended As Lovers, which helped Beck achieve success with his album Blow by Blow in 1975.

The lyrics of Superstition explore common superstitions, such as the number 13, broken mirrors, or walking under a ladder, emphasizing the foolishness underlying such beliefs. According to Wonder, those who behave superstitiously only harm themselves, amplifying the negative effects of anything that might happen to them.

Yet, neither the anecdote nor the lyrics are the most interesting aspects of the song.

A Look Back at Stevie Wonder's Life
Stevland Judkins Morris was born in Michigan in May 1950 and became blind in his first days of life due to excessive oxygen in the incubator.

As often happens in the best stories of resilience, Stevie overcame this seemingly insurmountable obstacle, showcasing his immense musical talent from a young age.

At four years old, he began singing in his church choir, and by nine, he could already play the piano, harmonica, and drums. At eleven, he made his recording debut.

In 1961, he signed his first contract with the Motown record label and changed his name to "Little Stevie Wonder."

Over the next two years, his first albums were released with mixed success: A Tribute to Uncle Ray and The Jazz Soul of Little Stevie. His breakthrough finally came with The 12 Year Old Genius and the harmonica-driven track Fingertips.

The single soared to the top of both pop and R&B charts, and The 12 Year Old Genius became Motown's best-selling album at the time.

Following several less successful singles, Stevie took a break to focus entirely on classical piano studies.

He returned in 1964, now known simply as Stevie Wonder, and quickly climbed the charts with Uptight (Everything's Alright) and later Too Good to My Baby.

In the following seven years, he accumulated more hits, such as Signed, Sealed, Delivered I'm Yours in collaboration with singer Syreeta Wright, whom he later married.

In 1971, with his Motown contract expiring and royalties from his trust fund becoming his sole property, Wonder released Where I'm Coming From, his first fully self-produced and self-composed album. Though it wasn't a commercial success, it marked a turning point.

Stevie renegotiated his contract with Motown, securing full rights to his music and complete control over his recordings.

This marked the beginning of his golden era.

In 1972, Music of My Mind epitomized Wonder's definitive rise to success with innovative musical experiments that immediately captivated audiences. From this album onward, Stevie decided to write, produce, arrange, and play nearly all his music independently.

This brings us back to Talking Book, the album containing Superstition. Its release was an extraordinary success, cementing Stevie Wonder as the undisputed king of Black music, highlighting his ability to blend revolutionary approaches with increasingly catchy melodies.

Stevie Wonder's journey is not a tale of talent alone but also of relentless dedication to mastering diverse skills. His ability to play instruments ranging from harmonica and drums to bass, percussion, piano, and synthesizers fueled his career.

Wonder's true breakthrough came when he learned to write, produce, and arrange music. If Stevie Wonder were divided into multiple micro-artists, each specializing in only one skill—playing, singing, writing, producing, or arranging—it's unlikely we would have seen the same creative impact he achieved as a whole.

Multidisciplinarity was the key to his success, making him stand out. His incredible talent, evident from a young age, reached its full potential because Wonder applied himself with total dedication to developing a well-rounded musical profile.

The Role of Multidisciplinarity in the Future of Work
Multidisciplinarity doesn't mean omniscience—an overwhelming and unnecessary goal.

In the near future, technical aspects of jobs will diminish in importance, leaving more room for soft skills. However, this doesn't mean technical knowledge will disappear entirely.

Take algorithms, for example, often viewed as mythical creatures operating independently. Yet, every algorithm, no matter how complex or automated, requires human oversight—algorithmic governance.

This governance is often exercised by non-technical professionals. For instance, in search engines, legal experts play a critical role in ensuring compliance with privacy laws.

While a lawyer doesn't need to be a programmer, they must understand basic algorithmic principles to be effective. This is multidisciplinarity.

In the future, every professional will need to develop "T-shaped" skills—deep expertise in their core field combined with a broad, shallow understanding of adjacent areas.

This doesn't require multiple degrees or specialized courses but rather curiosity—the essential ingredient for a multidisciplinary approach. Asking questions, seeking information, and exploring topics are the primary ways to implement it.

A multidisciplinary approach fosters lateral thinking, solving problems in one field by drawing on knowledge from another, even if seemingly unrelated. It activates "connecting the dots" reasoning, as Steve Jobs famously advocated, enabling unexpected solutions to emerge by integrating insights from diverse areas.

Stevie Wonder made multidisciplinarity his creed, and year after year, it rewarded him for his efforts. Had he been a "lazy" artist, content to rest on the laurels of his early talent, the world would have missed out on his sublime musicality and unique lyrics—the fruits of his phenomenal multidisciplinarity.

Track #9: Get Back, Stress and Conflict Management

"Get back, get back. Get back to where you once belonged. Get back Jojo, go home" — Beatles.

Get Back, one of the countless Beatles' hits, holds a special meaning for the band and its fans.
The song, written by John Lennon and Paul McCartney, was released as a single in April 1969 and later included, slightly revised, as the final track of the Let It Be album in 1970.

It is often considered the Beatles' final song, and its lyrics seem to echo what fans would have wished to say to the band members after their split: "Come back home!"
The story behind the creation of this last album by the most famous band of all time speaks of a group fraught with tensions, in total crisis, unwilling to organize concerts or perform live for years.

The only exception was their last performance on a rooftop, where Get Back closed the improvised setlist. This makes it the last song ever played by the Beatles in concert, back in 1969.

Since their final concert in San Francisco in 1966, the band seemed inclined to avoid large live performances despite the fame they had brought them. However, no official statement regarding this decision had been made by the band or their entourage.
Among the four, Paul McCartney missed the thrill of live shows the most and proposed a bold idea: a grand concert filmed entirely for a movie.

While John Lennon and Ringo Starr welcomed the idea enthusiastically, George Harrison was less keen.
The challenge lay in choosing the right location—an epic, unique outdoor venue to make the event one-of-a-kind, a show unmatched by any group or artist in the future.
Suggestions ranged from the Egyptian pyramids to cruise liners.

While deciding on the venue, the band began shooting behind-the-scenes footage at Twickenham Studios in early January 1969.

The result? A total relational disaster.
Only Paul arrived on time and engaged actively in the project, while the others oscillated between delays and unannounced absences.
What was once a harmonious group built on chemistry had become four reluctant soloists imposing their preferences on each other.

One day, George, feeling marginalized, clashed harshly with Paul during filming and, reportedly, came to blows with John off-camera. The shooting was halted, and George walked off the set.
The band relocated to Apple Studios, though George was on the verge of quitting the Beatles altogether after the arguments.

They eventually began working on a new album, featuring raw music without stylistic embellishments like overdubs or edits, aiming to return to their roots—Get Back.

Still, the idea of a grand concert lingered until someone casually suggested the rooftop of their record label.

Despite the cold, foggy weather and the reluctance of George and Ringo, John Lennon famously said, "Let's do it," and the band took to the rooftop.

Thus, around noon on January 30, 1969, the Beatles' final live performance took place—the iconic Rooftop Concert.

Initially, a moderate commotion stirred below the building and in the neighborhood as news spread of the impromptu concert. Crowds soon swelled, with people gathering on the streets, balconies, and rooftops.

Despite police intervention to shut down the performance, the Beatles continued playing for another mesmerizing half-hour.
During Get Back, Paul McCartney improvised lyrics mocking the situation:
"You've been playing on the roof again, and that's no good. You know your Mummy doesn't like that... she's gonna have you arrested! Get back!"

The concert ended with Get Back and John Lennon quipping: "I'd like to say thank you on behalf of the group and ourselves, and I hope we've passed the audition."

Though it seemed like a triumphant new beginning, it marked the band's final act.
The Beatles, plagued by unresolved conflicts, both internal and external, and the stress of their immense success, were at breaking point.
Greedy manager Allen Klein, Yoko Ono's influence, and diverging artistic tastes were just a few factors contributing to the Fab Four's demise.

A pivotal turning point was the death of their longtime manager Brian Epstein, who had been their biggest fan. His loss dealt a severe blow to the band, and Paul McCartney later identified it as the main reason for their eventual breakup.

Allen Klein entered the picture through John Lennon, who handed him complete control of his affairs shortly after meeting him—much to the dismay of the other Beatles. Klein and Ono, with their assertive personalities, disrupted the band's fragile balance, hastening their disbandment.

The Beatles were unprepared to manage the stress and conflicts that came with their transition from carefree musicians to a high-pressure business enterprise.

Managing Stress and Conflict in the Workplace
In today's volatile work environment, stress and conflict management are increasingly vital skills. The workplace is becoming more turbulent, with constant structural and contextual changes leading to uncertainty, stress, and conflict.

Dave Snowden's Cynefin Framework offers a useful reference for navigating such challenges, categorizing work contexts into four types:

Stable: Activities follow simple cause-effect relationships that can be categorized and proceduralized.
Complicated: Problems are harder to analyze, requiring case-by-case solutions.
Complex: Involves unknown variables and requires agile processes to adapt to rapid changes.
Chaotic: No predictable outcomes; decisions rely on intuition and courage.
As workplaces increasingly resemble complex and chaotic contexts, success depends on agile approaches to uncertainty. Stress and conflicts become inevitable, requiring emotional resilience and adaptive strategies.

The Beatles' inability to manage stress and conflicts with resilience ultimately led to their breakup. Had they navigated these challenges rationally, setting aside personal grievances, their story might have continued longer, adding more immortal hits to their legacy.

As professionals, developing resilience, embracing agility, and managing conflicts objectively can turn even the most challenging situations into opportunities for growth and success—both personal and collective.

Track #10: Come as You Are, Empathy

"Come as you are. As you were. As I want you to be. As a friend. As a friend. As an old enemy." - Nirvana

Kurt Cobain, iconic frontman of Nirvana, is part of the infamous "27 Club," a group of prominent singers and artists who passed away at the young age of 27.
The causes of death often include alcohol or drug abuse, accidents, suicide, or even unusual causes like poisoning.
Jimi Hendrix, Jim Morrison, and Amy Winehouse—the most recent addition—are just some of the names on this haunting list.

Cobain's death occurred on April 5, 1994, in his Lake Washington home near Seattle, but his body was not discovered until three days later. Found lifeless alongside a farewell note and a shotgun, the conclusion was that he had taken his own life.
Theories surrounding his death are plentiful, with the most popular being a conspiracy that he was murdered. However, no evidence has ever disproven the official ruling of suicide.
What is clear is that Kurt Cobain was not suited to the star lifestyle that gradually consumed and extinguished him.

The note Cobain wrote shortly before his death, though open to various interpretations, unequivocally reveals a man unable to feel emotions—a life scarred despite global success.
The words he left as his final goodbye are heartbreakingly addressed to Boddah, his imaginary friend who had been with him all his life.
Among Cobain's last words was a Neil Young lyric: "It's better to burn out than fade away." Since then, every time Young performs My My, Hey Hey, he dedicates another of his lyrics to the late artist, emphasizing the line: "Once you're gone, you can't come back."

The essence of Cobain's farewell, however, is encapsulated in three words: peace, love, empathy. These words, which conclude his letter, are not random but represent what life meant to Kurt.
Peace and love are themes we can discuss endlessly—found in poems, songs, revolutions, and wars, they are simultaneously humanity's goal and its driving force.
But empathy is rarely discussed in artistic works, even though it was foundational for Cobain.

For years, the artist was labeled the epitome of excess, drug and alcohol abuse, and unscrupulous behavior with a single goal: profit.
Only posthumously has it become apparent that this was merely a mask—perhaps not even one he chose to wear—behind which Kurt found himself trapped.
Cobain possessed extraordinary empathy for others, yet struggled to manage it, feeding his emotional fragility.
His final words clearly show his ability to put himself in others' shoes, a burden of unbearable suffering.

The Nirvana frontman's essence was enigmatic, entirely consumed by a musical mission that seemed almost divinely assigned. His obsessive intensity permeated every aspect of his life.
In his songs, Kurt tried to cry out against societal dynamics, drowning his thoughts in drugs to escape what others couldn't—or wouldn't—see or understand.
His true purpose was almost the opposite of what the world perceived: a stark provocation beyond any conventional framework.
All he wanted was to be himself, as expressed in one of his most famous songs, Come as You Are.

Come as You Are is the second single from the album Nevermind. Its unmistakable rhythm is instantly recognizable to anyone with even a modicum of musical knowledge.

Behind the track lies a string of anecdotes, including a plagiarism lawsuit by the British rock band Killing Joke. The intro to Come as You Are is strikingly similar to their song Eighties.

Even Cobain himself expressed reservations about releasing it as a single, due to its similarity to the British band's track. However, Cobain's untimely death led Killing Joke to drop the lawsuit.

Released in 1992, the song has inspired various interpretations regarding its meaning and origins. Charles R. Cross, in his book Here We Are Now, suggests that Kurt was inspired by the Morck Hotel in Aberdeen, whose slogan was "Come as You Are." Allegedly, Cobain visited this hotel during his time as a homeless man.

Regardless of its origins, Cobain explained that the song speaks about people and the expectations placed upon them.

The eclectic frontman felt overwhelmingly judged throughout his brief life—a paradox, as Kurt placed empathy at the center of his relationships, driven by sincere interest in others' feelings and experiences.

This attitude, starkly at odds with how the world viewed him, may have been his undoing.

Cobain knew his fans would die for him, yet he also understood that his actions no longer aligned with what gave his life meaning.

In his letter, he wrote:

"The fact is, I can't fool you, any of you. It simply wouldn't be right for you or for me. The worst crime I can think of would be to pretend and fake enjoyment 100% of the time. Sometimes I feel like I have to clock in whenever I step on stage. I've tried everything in my power to appreciate this. I appreciated the fact that I and the others have affected and entertained so many people. But I must be one of those narcissists who only appreciates things once they're gone. I'm too sensitive. I need to be slightly numbed to regain the enthusiasm I once had as a child."

His sensitivity, combined with his rock-star status, may have burst the fragile bubble that protected Kurt, driving him to the edge.

Ironically, Cobain may not have died from excessive empathy, but from the world's complete lack of empathy toward him.

Empathy can save lives. It can also propel today's and tomorrow's professionals toward success. Its etymology—en-pathos (Greek for "feeling inside")—reflects its essence: the ability to experience another person's emotions as if they were your own.

Empathy facilitates genuine connection and understanding of others, breaking down barriers and building stronger relationships.

Empathy can be innate but can also be cultivated with practice—by listening, asking questions, and showing genuine interest in others. Far from mystical advice, these are scientifically-backed activities involving mirror neurons, which allow us to resonate with others' emotions.

In professional environments, empathy enables innovative problem-solving, diffuses conflict, and anticipates challenges. As Freud once suggested, empathy is the key to understanding the psyche of others—a principle now recognized as vital in modern workplaces.

Perhaps, had the world shown more empathy for Kurt Cobain, we might still be enjoying his unparalleled musical genius.

The Virtuous Contamination

Being able to navigate the evolution of work that the world is currently experiencing is not, and will not be, a task for the few.
Each of us, at varying levels of complexity, will have to face the evolution of markets, competitive environments, organizational structures, and ultimately, the skills required.

The greatest challenge most of us will encounter won't be learning new skills but rather unlearning old ones.
Our organizational behaviors stem from a blend of experiences and aptitudes that, over time, have shaped the defining contours of our professional identities.
Stepping outside these contours isn't easy—it means questioning the very paradigms that have driven us to where we are today, whether we like it or not, and that have defined our careers, for better or worse.

But now is the time.

The critical factor that will determine professional evolution or stagnation lies in the mindset we adopt.
Those who embrace this change wholeheartedly will be able to ride a wave that is only beginning to swell; those who hesitate will eventually need to catch up. But waiting will mean watching that wave grow until it becomes nearly impossible to ride.

The mindset needed to make this leap cannot exist without a renewal of our skills. For the fortunate (or simply the pioneers), this will be an evolution—a step up.
To renew ourselves, as previously mentioned, we must know how to unlearn, how to question everything we once considered unshakable truths.
But in the future world of work, there will unfortunately be no room for such unshakable certainties.

Our approach will need to adapt to coexist with an increasingly volatile world—volatile in structure and content—where, yes, technology will reign supreme, but where the role of people will be equally indispensable.
Unlearning, evolving, and adapting are the three key principles that will determine who will succeed and who will not.

These concepts might seem disconnected and even further removed from the skills we've considered so far, but that's not the case.
There is a close relationship between these three elements, between skills, and between the elements and the skills themselves.
Each enables the other and vice versa.

This may seem complex to manage, but here's perhaps the best news:
Working on one skill already lays the foundation for developing another or others. All are interconnected because they stem from the same fundamental mindset.

Empathy is the foundation of emotional intelligence and is a valuable asset in managing diversity and inclusivity. Working on creativity generates virtuous dynamics that can enhance our complex problem-solving or storytelling abilities, dynamics that are also positively influenced by multidisciplinarity.

Learning to manage change effectively drastically reduces stress and allows for prudent conflict management.
And so on.

It all starts with addressing one area of focus; the rest will follow almost naturally.

A few years ago, before my first public speech in front of a corporate audience of about 500 people, I asked an English Vice President of my then-company, who was visiting the Italian branch, for advice.
The advice was disarmingly simple, almost veering into banality: memorize only the first sentence; the rest will flow naturally, guided by the key points you already know you need to cover.

Well, I've carried this advice with me ever since, cherished it, and applied it—not just for public speeches but also in other areas, adapting its underlying principle.
The key is to break the ice.

In this context, breaking the ice means starting to work on your professional self in a concrete and practical way, focusing on the skills that, even with a superficial analysis, seem most relevant to your field now and in the future.
Yes, a superficial analysis—because all skills will be essential, albeit with varying weights.

But the important thing is to break the ice.

The beauty of soft skills is that they are rooted in behaviors, which influence one another and, in turn, influence others' behaviors toward us.
Adopting a mindset open to change and continuous skill development can create a virtuous circle within your professional dimension, positively impacting how others interact with you.

This is the essence of virtuous contamination.

If someone on a team decides to "break the ice" and experiment with one or another soft skill, it's not just they who will benefit—and not just from that single skill. Instead, a process of contamination will begin, through which they will unknowingly start to develop other skills as well, and the entire team will benefit from this change, encouraging everyone to break the ice in turn.

Shifting from a "micro" approach, focused on the individual, to a "macro" one, centered on the organization, we can see that many companies are already striving—and will increasingly strive—to foster these dynamics within their structures.
These dynamics lead to personal growth for employees and greater well-being in the workplace, triggering internal entrepreneurship dynamics that enable organizations to confidently face increasing volatility and dynamism.

The equation, in this case, is straightforward: mastering the future context will equate to success.

Returning from the "macro" to the "micro": companies will increasingly aim for this, meaning the people called to lead critical business processes and projects will be those who have already embraced these dynamics as their professional mantra. Let's call them "contaminators."

It almost seems like a linear process, but it's anything but.
It's a matter of daily practical training, made up of trials and, above all, failures.

Embracing this new mindset, even if it means standing out today as a black sheep among a flock of orderly white ones, can give you a distinctive competitive advantage over other professionals tomorrow.

Organizational behaviors in general—and more specifically soft skills—are no longer and will no longer be optional. They are a must-have.

So, what are you waiting for to break the ice?

www.ingramcontent.com/pod-product-compliance
Lightning Source LLC
Chambersburg PA
CBHW030042230526
45472CB00005B/1644